REAL life GUIDES

CARE, WELFARE & COMMUNITY WORK

2ND EDITION

CAROLINE BARKER & CAMILLA ZAJAC

Real Life Guide to Care, Welfare & Community Work

This second edition published in 2010 by Trotman, an imprint
of Crimson Publishing, Westminster House, Kew Road,
Richmond, Surrey TW9 2ND

© Trotman Publishing 2010

Authors of this second edition: Caroline Barker and
Camilla Zajac

Author of first edition: Emma Caprez

© Trotman Publishing 2010
First edition published by Trotman & Co Ltd 2006
© Trotman & Co Ltd 2006

British Library Cataloguing in Publication Data
A catalogue record for this book is available from the British
Library

ISBN: 978-1-84455-233-7

Typeset by IDSUK (DataConnection) Ltd
Printed and bound by CPI Antony Rowe, Chippenham, Wiltshire

CONTENTS

About the authors   v

Acknowledgements   vi

Foreword   vii

Introduction   ix

Chapter 1   **Success story**   1

Chapter 2   **What is care, welfare and
             community work?**   7

Chapter 3   **What are the jobs?**   21

Chapter 4   **Real lives 1**   37

Chapter 5   **Tools of the trade**   41

Chapter 6   **FAQs**   51

Chapter 7   **Real lives 2**   61

Chapter 8   **Training and qualifications**   65

Chapter 9   **Real lives 3**   81

Chapter 10   **The last word**   85

Chapter 11   **Further information**   89

Chapter 12   **Jargon busters**   101

ABOUT THE AUTHORS

CAROLINE BARKER

Caroline Barker is a professionally qualified careers adviser with many years' experience of providing careers guidance and counselling to a wide range of clients. She has worked with school pupils, apprenticeship trainees, college students, and adults seeking a career change. Her work at present is predominantly geared towards young people. She is committed to producing accurate and engaging careers information for this readership, enabling them to make informed choices about their future careers.

Caroline is also the author of *Real Life Guide: Police Service* and *Real Life Guide: Childcare* both published by Trotman.

CAMILLA ZAJAC

Camilla Zajac developed her role as a freelance careers writer whilst working in communications in the statutory and voluntary sectors. She wrote for a wide range of careers resources aimed at young people, students and adults. Six years ago Camilla set up her own copywriting business and since then has written for communications and resources in the careers and business sectors.

Camilla is also the author of *Real Life Guide: Working Outdoors* and she has co-authored *Real Life Guide: Hospitality & Events Management,* both published by Trotman.

ACKNOWLEDGEMENTS

Many thanks to Zoe Benton, Alison Pennington and Steve Sutton for originally agreeing to be interviewed and give up their time, and to my husband Nick who, being a social worker, was a great source of advice and information in terms of researching careers in the social care sector.
Caroline Barker

Many thanks to Grace Easie-Edgar for sharing her time and experience.
Camilla Zajac

FOREWORD

**Are you looking for a rewarding, long-term career in a growing sector?
Social care could be the answer.**

There are many routes into social care, allowing you to develop your own unique career path to suit your needs and ambitions including enhancing your current skills as well as gaining new ones.

Social care is a growing sector with many diverse roles. People are living longer and have a right to live their lives how they choose, with greater independence and choice. If you choose to work in social care, you will be offering to help people with a whole range of different requirements. You could be giving support to people with learning disabilities or who are older. You could be helping people to live independently in their own homes or caring for people living in residential settings.

No two days are the same in social care! Job variety, flexible hours and the satisfaction from helping others are what drive many social care staff forward.

For more information about working in social care visit

www.skillsforcare.org.uk/apprenticeships

Post-16 Apprenticeships are open to all ages above 16. Whilst employers have their own recruitment criteria, notably CRB checks, apprentices also must be employed a minimum of 16 hours per week.

INTRODUCTION

Adult social care, welfare and community work is one of the largest sectors in the country. It is also one of the fastest growing parts of the economy. High-profile news stories and concerns about the future of social care mean that this sector is frequently in the spotlight. It is a sector that is growing in terms of careers, training and qualifications. In this book you can find out what working in social care, welfare and community work involves and how to start your career in this area.

You might be surprised to find out just how varied the social care, welfare and community sector is. Every day, professionals working in this area make an important difference to people's lives. The roles vary widely – as do the work settings.

In Chapters 4, 7 and 9 you can read about real professionals from the social sector. They share their stories and offer you tips and advice on making your own career a brilliant success.

Let's have a look at what else is coming up in the book.

▶ **Chapter 1: Success story** Read about Grace Easie-Edgar, who has made a fantastic career for herself in the care sector. If you're ambitious and driven to succeed in your career, Grace's inspirational story and her tips and advice will help you start planning your future right now.

▶ **Chapter 2: What is care, welfare and community work?** This chapter looks at the sector as a whole and its value to many different people. You will also find out about government plans to develop social care and what this means for jobs and training.

▶ **Chapter 3: What are the jobs?** In this chapter you can learn in detail about the different roles available in the sector. From working out in the community to helping people in their homes, this area offers a variety of job opportunities. This chapter should help you to think about which role might suit you.

▶ **Chapter 5: Tools of the trade** How are your people skills? In this sector a positive, professional approach is vital. In this chapter you can see the kinds of skills and personal qualities it takes to succeed in this sector and how to improve your own.

▶ **Chapter 6: FAQs** This chapter answers all your burning questions, about everything from hours and pay to promotion and career development.

▶ **Chapter 8: Training and qualifications** Now you know more about the sector, but how do you get into it? This chapter outlines what you need to study to get a job in social care, welfare and community work. You can also find out how you can gain valuable skills and qualifications when you've started working.

▶ **Chapter 10: The last word** Have a go at the light-hearted quiz, which can help you decide if this is the right career choice for you.

▶ **Chapter 11: Further information** In this chapter you will find details of useful organisations and publications so that you can find out lots more about this sector and begin job searching.

▶ **Chapter 12: Jargon busters** Don't know what a word or phrase means? Turn to this chapter to find out.

CHAPTER 1
SUCCESS STORY

Vital Stats: Grace Easie-Edgar

First job: Trainee residential childcare officer
Career high point: Meeting the Queen and going to the Women of the Year event

You will read in Grace's story her background in child social care, something which isn't covered in this book but which you can find out more about in the *Real Life Guide to Childcare*. However, Grace now works with a team of adult professionals providing advice and guidance. This success story emphasises the fact that while working in child social care and adult social care are very different roles, social workers in both sectors can progress into management roles where they will be supporting teams of professionals. Read about other professionals working directly with adults in the other case studies in this book.

Grace Easie-Edgar is Operations Manager for Birmingham City Council's Leaving Care service. She is responsible for supporting more than 700 young people previously in the care of Birmingham Council to help them access accommodation, employment and training opportunities and to help them to live independently.

Grace is very proud to have recently become the first African Caribbean woman to be elected to the post of

President of the Social Care Association, the professional body for social care workers. In addition to this, Grace is also a leading member of the Black Managers Forum, having previously been executive member and secretary.

> **❝** Identify positive role models and be clear about your ambitions and aspirations. **❞**

Grace started out wanting to be a nurse after leaving school at the age of 16. But after realising the training took too long, she responded to an opportunity to work for Birmingham City Council as a trainee residential childcare officer.

Grace's passion for the work meant she quickly moved up to management level, going on to run a residential establishment for the first time. After completing her Diploma in Social Work, Grace gained qualified social worker status in 1985.

She left the local authority and moved into the voluntary sector, running an independent children's home for five years. Later on, she went back into the local authority as a team manager before progressing into her current job as operations manager.

Grace's demanding role involves supporting a range of professionals who work with young people leaving care – from team managers to aftercare advisers.

She also works regularly with partner agencies, including Connexions services, housing advisers and training organisations, to make sure that young people's training, employment and development needs are met – all with the aim of helping them to achieve their independence and move ahead with their lives. Grace has also found the time to fit in additional management qualifications, such as an MA in Social Services Management.

> **“** I have made the most of every opportunity to work with young people. I want to leave them something positive to think about. Ultimately it is about making a positive change. **”**

As well as her main job, Grace will now be involved in leading the Social Care Association, the national body that represents professionals across the social care sector. For Grace, her election into this new role is 'overwhelming and exciting'. Her new position has already led to her meeting the Queen and attending the prestigious Women of the Year event!

Grace has proved the potential for moving ahead in this sector. So what would she say to a young person hoping to get into social care?

'Look out for relevant volunteering opportunities and also look at what relevant life experience you have. Identify positive role models and be clear about your ambitions and aspirations.'

Finally, what is Grace's secret to achieving so much in her career – and what has kept her motivated?

'I want to help change people's lives. I have made the most of every opportunity to work with young people. I want to leave them something positive to think about. Ultimately it is about making a positive change.'

Grace's top tip
“ If you want to work in this sector, stay focused on your goals and be confident. **”**

SCA Case Study

Jim, from Mechanic to Care Manager

Jim has severe dyslexia – he left school as soon as he could and began work as a mechanic. He was very unhappy in this role, feeling unfulfilled and dissatisfied. A friend suggested that he should try some voluntary work in a local resource centre for learning disability.

Following this volunteering experience Jim became a 1:1 worker with someone with learning disabilities.

He decided to become more qualified, started his NVQ training, and worked closely with an assessor and a mentor who understood his dyslexia and provided resources in media other than the written word. The assessor, recognizing the potential difficulties for Jim in writing all his material, ensured that he had access to a computer with voice recognition software and used critical discussion and questioning to assess his knowledge.

His employer gave Jim additional time to complete his work and although much needed to be completed in his own time, with the support of these key people, Jim successfully completed his qualification.

However, he felt that there must be much more that he could do and that there had to be more to life than working for the PCT. He also felt that his own experience of being supported could be a starting point for bigger things.

He bought a house and made it into a home for people with learning disabilities. Having set that up and got it established as a positive resource, which is both well run and offers a good service, Jim has now begun to provide domiciliary care service.

The Social Care Association

Social Care Association was founded in 1949 as the House Parents Association for staff working in Children's Homes.

1.5 million care workers deliver a range of support, care and assistance to 3 million people over 24 hours a day and 365 days a year at a generally competent and good quality level.

SCA was founded to promote good practice in social care, first by providing a network of like minded professionals who could talk to each other about the challenges and opportunities of their privileged day to day work. This work then expanded to writing good practice guidance that could be shared in groups to disseminate this knowledge.

In 1984, The charity SCA (Education) was founded to provide direct training to care workers who were largely unqualified for the task and for whom, there was no structured qualification.

The Associations lobbied for national standards, worker registration and qualification, all to raise the standard of care and the level of public trust.

More recently with the fragmentation of social care provision to about 35,000 different companies and a quarter of a million Direct Payment users, SCA has been involved in supporting workers in a range of issues to ensure the best outcome for service users.

CHAPTER 2
WHAT IS CARE, WELFARE AND COMMUNITY WORK?

THE SOCIAL CARE SECTOR

What is the social care sector?

As you read on, you will come across the term 'social care sector'. This is the umbrella term given to all jobs in the three areas we will explore in this book: adult care, welfare and community work.

Why do we need social care?

We all have additional needs at different stages of life. Adult care, welfare and community jobs are about practical (and sometimes emotional) support that benefits people. Social care helps to meet the needs of the most vulnerable groups in our society, such as elderly people and people with special needs, so that they can access the services they're entitled to.

In the past, the sector has suffered from a negative image because of a number of high-profile cases in the news, mainly to do with the treatment and care of clients or service users. It has also been negatively affected by a high turnover of staff due to the temporary or short-term nature of many care roles and to the relatively low wages.

⚡ NEWSFLASH!

In the next 20 years the number of people aged over 85 in England will double.

Adult social care is big news at the moment. This is because there is a greater need than ever before to have a high standard of social care in this country.

This sector relies on motivated and enthusiastic people who are dedicated to helping others have the best possible quality of life. Whatever area you choose to work in, you'll find your role involves offering support to people. They could be individuals who are moving from homelessness into their own accommodation, or people looking to deal with debt problems, to name only two.

LEARN THE LINGO

Don't know what a word means? Turn to the Jargon Busters chapter on page 99 to find out.

Your role could even involve helping groups of people, for example in a community development role. Compassion and sensitivity are therefore extremely important qualities if you're considering a career in this area.

The social care sector: then and now

The British Welfare State from 1945 to 1979

After the Second World War, the government realised that changes needed to be made to deal with issues such as poverty and deprivation. In 1942, the Liberal politician William Beveridge identified the five main problems that needed to be tackled: poverty, disease, ignorance, squalor, idleness. To deal with these, he proposed setting up a welfare state with social security, a national health service, free education, council housing and full employment. The new welfare state led to the following developments.

▶ **Free education.** The school leaving age was set to the age of 15 years old to make sure that children received a basic education.

▶ **Social security.** People who were unemployed could now receive unemployment pay for six months. They could also receive sick pay for as long as they were ill. The new system also provided benefits for anyone who was considered to be 'in need'.

▶ **Full employment.** The government wanted to get industry healthy again after the war, so they increased public spending and nationalised road haulage, the railways and the coal and steel industries.

▶ **Council housing.** Councils now had to provide good housing and care for all children 'deprived of a normal home life'. The government set itself a target of building 300,000 new houses a year and 1.25 million council houses were built between 1945 and 1951.

▶ **National Health Service.** After the National Health Service was introduced in 1948, the following services were available free to everyone: doctors, hospitals, opticians, dentists, ambulances, health visitors and midwives.

Welfare from 1979 to 1997

During this time, benefits were reduced and many welfare payments were limited. The levels of tax people had to pay were also reduced.

Welfare since 1997

Public spending has increased through higher levels of tax. Benefits are now targeted towards people who need more support, such as children and pensioners.

⚡ NEWSFLASH!

The origins of the welfare state in the UK go right back to Elizabethan times when the Poor Laws were introduced to help make sure that poor people had enough to live on.

In 2005, social care in England was separated into children's social care services and adult social care services. This was to ensure that both groups of people were supported in the best way possible to meet all of their individual needs.

The social care sector today

January 2006: the government publishes a White Paper, *Our Health, Our Care, Our Say: A New Direction for Community Services.*

This report explained how the government planned to improve the way social care services work. It aimed to do this by providing people with good quality social care and NHS services in their local communities. The intention was to help make social care services more personalised to suit different people's needs.

December 2007: the government publishes the report *Putting People First: A Shared Vision and Commitment to the Transformation of Adult Social Care.*

This explained how the government planned to change the way adult social care services work by making them more flexible and varied. A big part of this was to make sure the sector had all the employees it needed – with the right skills.

May 2008: the government publishes *The Case for Change: Why England Needs a New Care and Support System*.

The report looked at why it is so important that the social care system changes. This is vital because people are living longer and will need more care and support in the future. The government asked members of the public and organisations how they would like the care and support system to change.

July 2009: the government publishes *Shaping the Future of Care Together*.

This report launched the big care debate – the very first national debate about changing adult care and support in England. The new report also looked at exactly how a national care service would work. The government asked people for their feedback on this by November 2009.

The future of social care

Social care has to develop. People are living longer and we need professional support and funding to support an older population. As life expectancy increases, many people are spending longer periods of their lives with a disability or a long-term condition.

> **66** The sector also has to provide support for people with different needs. **99**

WHAT DOES THIS MEAN FOR THE FUTURE OF SOCIAL CARE CAREERS?

As the social care sector develops, improved job and career development opportunities are becoming more widely available.

▶ **More training and support:** in the future, people working in the sector will have more training and development options, thanks to the launch of the National Skills Academy for Social Care.

▶ **More Apprenticeships:** there are set to be more opportunities to work and gain skills in social care. The government wants to create 50,000 new social care Apprenticeships. The scheme that was to do this is curently under review.

▶ **More opportunities:** the government wants more people to look at a career in this sector and is to launch an annual national recruitment campaign to let people know what opportunities are available.

▶ **More local information:** there will be more ways for people to learn about opportunities to work in social care through their local community.

> ❝ The government wants more people to look at a career in this sector. ❞

SO WHAT ABOUT THE INDIVIDUAL PARTS OF THE SECTOR?

The table below gives an overview of what sort of jobs people do in this sector.

	Who does it help?	Where?	How does it help?	Issues?
Adult social care	Wide range of client groups, from young adults to elderly people.	In people's homes, in residential homes.	Providing support with everyday living and maintaining independence.	Personal care, mobility, rehabilitation (e.g. after leaving hospital).
Welfare	People of all ages who need help, advice or support.	In advice centres based in towns or on an outreach basis in local communities.	Delivering advice in centres based in towns or in communities.	Debt, housing, benefits, unemployment, substance misuse.
Community	People of all ages in local communities.	In local communities.	Developing local communities to make them better places to live, learn and work.	Community safety, antisocial behaviour, community development.

Adult social care

▶ The adult social care sector helps many different people, from young adults with learning difficulties to elderly people. This is a sector that has an impact on many people's lives by providing services and support to help people to keep their independence and enjoy a better quality of life.

▶ Social care is made up of many different employers and organisations, from charities to local councils to private providers.

▶ This sector is changing because people are living longer. People are also looking to live more independently and stay in their own homes wherever possible.

▶ The government is increasing training opportunities and career routes.

Welfare

▶ Everyone needs additional support at some stage of their lives. The welfare sector provides much-needed advice and help to many people, whether they are looking to make a life-changing decision or simply need to be better informed about their choices.

> ### ⚡ NEWSFLASH!
>
> The *Big Issue* was launched in 1991 in direct response to the number of people sleeping rough on the streets of London, but it was also inspired by a newspaper called *Street News*, which was sold on the streets of New York.

▶ Welfare services focus on empowering people to improve their own lives, from advising clients on their employment options to helping people get out of debt.

▶ As with social care, employers vary across the sector. Welfare workers are employed by charities, local councils and specialist organisations.

Community

▶ Community work is a developing area. The government recognises how important it is to support local communities and is funding new projects.

▶ The community sector helps local areas to empower themselves. Community development workers build on the strengths of a local area.

▶ Work that deals directly with issues such as antisocial behaviour has led to more community safety initiatives and more community safety professionals.

▶ It is likely that there will be more opportunities in this sector in the near future.

In a diverse job area such as social care, employers vary widely and the demand for professionals is growing.

Now have a go at the following quiz to see just how much you know about the social care sector.

CARE, WELFARE AND ❓ COMMUNITY WORK QUIZ

How much do you know about the social care, welfare and community work sector? Test your knowledge and then check your answers.

---

1 **A PCSO is:**
- A. A Police Community Support Officer.
- B. A type of support service.
- C. A legal term in the social care sector.

---

2 **A money adviser provides support with:**
- A. Debt issues.
- B. The best way to save for a rainy day.
- C. Finding a good deal on a credit card.

---

3 **In social care, a CRB check is:**
- A. A pre-employment test to check your knowledge of the social care sector.
- B. A system for managing client care.
- C. Carried out to help prevent unsuitable people working with children and vulnerable adults.

4 **A personal assistant is:**

A. A person who supports social care workers with administrative tasks.

B. A person who gives their opinion on a client's personal life.

C. A person who works on a one-to-one basis with an individual to give them the support they need.

5 **'Bank work' is:**

A. Casual or flexible working.

B. Helping people with their money.

C. Working overtime.

6 **Domiciliary care is:**

A. A new form of care management.

B. Care that takes place in a special centre.

C. Providing people with support in their own homes.

7 **Community development workers work in:**

A. Community centres.

B. Local people's homes.

C. Local authorities.

8 **The minimum age for working in social care is:**

A. 16

B. Any age

C. 18

9 **Personalisation is:**

A. Providing personal support to an individual.

B. Working on a one-to-one basis with a person.

C. A new government approach to providing social care services.

10 **The 'third sector' refers to:**

A. Voluntary and charitable organisations.

B. A special government body.

C. A type of community space.

ANSWERS

1 **A** – Police Community Support Officers (PCSOs) support regular police officers in the community. They are employed and managed by the police force, but are there to tackle issues that don't require the experience or powers of police officers. Their job is to deal with problems, such as antisocial behaviour, affecting local areas and to help improve the community and reassure local residents. PCSOs were introduced in 2002 and numbers are expected to rise in the future.

2 **A** – Money advisers help people deal with a wide range of debt issues, from debts such as mortgage, rent, council tax, fuel, TV licence to unsecured lending such as credit card debt. Whilst money advisers in this sector offer support to people with many different needs, they do not provide advice on saving or financial products.

3 **C** – Care workers often work with people in vulnerable situations or who are physically frail and so all applicants for social care jobs must undergo pre-employment checks. One such check is carried out by the Criminal Records Bureau (CRB), which examines police records and, where necessary, information held by the Independent Safeguarding Authority. See www.crb.homeoffice.gov.uk for more details.

4 **C** – This is a relatively new role in social care. Personal assistants help people to live independently by providing them with individual support. The actual job will depend on the needs of the person being cared for, so activities could cover many different areas.

5 **A** – 'Bank work' means covering shifts in the workplace when someone is off sick or away. It involves being available on an 'as and when' basis. This way of working can be a helpful way of gaining practical experience of a specific type of social care role, for example residential support work.

6 **C** – Domiciliary care refers to home care or home help. Care workers help people who need additional help to maintain their independence by providing support to them in their own homes. Care workers help people with personal care needs, such as washing and getting dressed, and practical tasks, such as preparing meals and shopping.

7 **A, B and C** – Community development workers may work in one or all of these types of settings. They may be employed by local authorities, voluntary sector organisations, faith groups, community groups or housing associations.

8 **A and C** – While it is possible to work in some areas of social care from the age of 16 in supervised roles, in other areas, for example in residential children's homes, care workers/trainees have to be over 18 years of age. The regulatory body – the Care Quality Commission – has developed national minimum standards which are used to regulate the provision of service in several areas of social care.

9 **C** – Personalisation is the government's plan for providing social care services in the future. 'Personalisation is about giving people much more choice and control over their lives' (*Personalisation – A Rough Guide,* Sarah Carr, Social Care Institute for Excellence). Personalisation means a move away from the way services have been provided in the past towards individual budgets/payments.

10 **A** – The third sector is a 'generic collective name for charity, voluntary, community, non-government and campaigning organisations' (The Community Development Exchange). The third sector is made up of a wide range of organisations, from large national charities to small community organisations run by local people. Professionals in social care, welfare and community work may be employed within the third sector, or work with organisations within it.

As you will have seen, social care is a broad-ranging sector that has an impact on many people, from making a difference to local communities to helping individuals change their lives for the better.

You will have noticed that the history of social care goes back a long way and that it is going through some very important changes right now. These developments mean that there are likely to be even more opportunities in social care in the future. Read on to find out more about what it's like to work in this varied sector.

Quick recap!

✓ The UK's ageing population means that there are new opportunities being created all the time for people to work in adult social care.

✓ Compassion and sensitivity are key qualities you will need if you are considering a career in this sector.

✓ The government is currently funding a lot of new training schemes to get into this sector, which means there are fantastic opportunities available and you're almost guaranteed to find a job.

✓ Most of the jobs in this sector focus on helping people maintain a good level of independence and enjoy a good quality of life.

CHAPTER 3
WHAT ARE THE JOBS?

While the focus of this book is on jobs you can enter without higher-level qualifications, some of the jobs profiled, such as social worker and occupational therapist, have been added to show how you can progress your career, through further qualifications and training, into more specialised professional roles.

⚡ NEWSFLASH!

The Community Justice programme is an innovative scheme in which sentencing focuses on offenders making amends to the community and receiving help to deal with the issues that may have contributed to them committing a crime.

ADULT CARE

Social care workers

If you opt for a role as a social care worker, you would work with people who might need support in their everyday lives, for many different reasons.

These roles are undertaken in a variety of settings – from people's homes to residential centres to supporting clients when they're out and about, for example whilst shopping or socialising.

❝ Many of these jobs are physically demanding, as you may have to assist people by lifting and moving them. ❞

SOCIAL CARE WORKERS AND SOCIAL WORKERS: WHAT'S THE DIFFERENCE?

Social care workers tend to offer more help with personal care and usually do not require any qualifications when they start work, as they receive on-the-job training.

As social care workers progress with their careers they have the opportunity to gain qualifications, such as National Vocational Qualifications (NVQs), which allow them to take on more responsibilities. In some cases, qualifications and experience gained as a social carer entitle people to go on and study for a social work degree.

Social workers need a degree because they support people at a senior level. You can find out more about this and other jobs requiring higher-level qualifications in the table on pages 27–9.

Source: www.socialcarecareers.co.uk

A lot of the jobs also involve personal care (help with activities such as washing, dressing or going to the toilet), so a sensitive, mature approach is essential.

HOME CARE

Home care worker

In this role you would provide vital practical support and personal care to people with additional needs, such as elderly people or those with physical disabilities.

With your help they'll be able to stay living at home with as much independence as possible.

- ▶ You would spend most of your time visiting people in their homes and your role would probably include:
  - o personal care, such as help with washing, dressing, eating and drinking

- o helping with laundry, cleaning, and food preparation
- o helping with administrative tasks, such as paying bills.

▶ You would help with the small things that make an important difference, like getting up in the morning.

▶ The nature of the job means you'll need to be prepared to work in the evenings and at weekends.

▶ You could work in a home care team for a local authority adult services department or for a care agency. With experience and further qualifications you could become a senior home care worker and then a home care manager.

Personal assistant

▶ You would work on a one-to-one basis with an individual client in their own home. You would give them whatever practical help they need to live independently, depending on the nature of their disability.

▶ You would be employed directly by your client for a set number of hours per week.

Residential care

Residential care homes provide support to people, who, because of their age or a disability, need additional support.

▶ As a **care assistant** in a residential home you would get to know residents and provide support with essential everyday activities such as washing, dressing, making breakfast and doing exercises.

▶ You might become a **key worker** to a resident, working with them on a one-to-one basis to help them through each day. The focus of your role could be older people suffering from dementia and other mental illnesses, which could make your job emotionally demanding. You'll need to be prepared to work shifts, including nights. With further experience and qualifications you could get promotion, for example to team leader, deputy manager, and then to care home manager.

Residential warden

▶ You would be responsible for looking after accommodation for people who live independent lives but sometimes need extra support. The majority of wardens work in accommodation for older people, although some work in hostels for homeless people, ex-offenders or drug users.

▶ You could also be responsible for helping residents to settle in, drawing up support plans for residents, organising outings and social events, and supervising staff. You would also be responsible for health and safety and security in the accommodation.

▶ Older people in sheltered accommodation have an alarm fitted so that they can call the warden if there is an emergency, so you could be on call at any time of the day or night.

▶ As a **support worker** in a residential home for people with mental health issues or learning disabilities, you would encourage people to be as independent as possible.

▶ Your job would involve helping people to develop their practical skills, such as cooking, cleaning, shopping and looking after their finances.

▶ You would also encourage people to take up new activities and support them with socialising and taking some time out. This may involve trips, for example to the cinema or a bowling alley. Again, it is likely that you would work shifts including nights in this job.

Day care

▶ Day care assistants work in day centres helping people to get involved in activities, learn new skills in a safe and supportive environment, and mix with other people.

▶ You might involve people in a wide range of indoor activities, from playing music to doing yoga.

▶ With experience and further qualifications you could take on more responsibilities and eventually become a day centre manager.

WELFARE

Advice and guidance

Advice worker

▶ You would provide free advice to people on a wide range of issues. Some advice workers offer general guidance in a number of areas such as debt, housing, employment,

⚡ NEWSFLASH!

Actress Samantha Morton and musician Goldie were both looked-after children when they were young. In 2009 the two celebrities helped to raise awareness of the important role that social workers play in a government campaign aimed at increasing the number of people going into this career.

EXPLODE THAT MYTH!
Carers are there to do everything for their clients
It's important to remember that as a care worker your main focus is on assisting your client to maintain their independence wherever possible. This means you need to know exactly what tasks you can take on to allow your client to carry on living their lives the way they want to.

welfare and education, while others specialise in a specific area.

▶ Whether you specialise or not, your work would involve interviewing people and helping them decide on the best course of action for them. You would also refer people to other sources of help, for example solicitors or social workers.

▶ Local authorities, advice centres, health services and voluntary organisations employ advice workers.

Debt adviser

▶ You would provide advice and guidance to people with debt problems. You might be helping people who have fallen behind with loan or mortgage repayments, or who are finding it difficult to meet their credit commitments.

▶ You would interview people to assess their financial situation, help people plan and manage their budgets, and negotiate on behalf of a client, for example a new payment schedule for a debt.

▶ Senior debt advisers also act as legal mediators for clients facing court action over their debt.

▶ You could work for an advice centre or in a specialist Money Advice Support Unit.

Welfare rights adviser

▶ Your job would involve advising clients on a wide range of benefits and welfare entitlements including social security benefits, housing benefits and tax credits.

▶ You would help clients to complete claim forms, and prepare appeals against decisions to stop benefits.

▶ You could work in an advice centre or for a local authority.

Adult guidance worker

▶ Your job would involve offering information, advice and guidance (IAG) to people about education, training and work opportunities. You might work with unemployed people, people who have been made redundant or people seeking a career change.

▶ You would interview people using counselling skills to help them make decisions. You might also help people to write CVs, improve their interview skills and apply for jobs.

▶ You could work for a careers company such as Connexions or for Jobcentre Plus.

▶ Opportunities in this area are growing and the government plans to launch a new adult advancement and careers service, open to everyone aged over 20, in 2010.

LEARN THE LINGO
Don't know what a word means? Turn to the Jargon Busters chapter on page 99 to find out.

Rehabilitation

Rehabilitation officer (hearing impairment)

▶ You would assess people with hearing impairments and advise them on special equipment, such as flashing-light doorbells and amplifiers for telephones, which would make their everyday activities easier.

▶ You would also advise people on ways of coping with their deafness and about getting the best use from their hearing aids. You might also refer people to other sources of help and support, for example voluntary organisations and health services.

▶ You could work for a local authority or in the third sector.

Rehabilitation officer (visual impairment)

▶ You would help people who have lost some or all of their vision to learn new ways of doing things such as cooking, cleaning and personal care. This would involve teaching safe ways to move about indoors and outdoors.

▶ You would also provide information on specialist equipment such as adapted computers and magnifying aids, and on the availability of financial and other sources of help. You would also help people to cope emotionally with their new situation.

▶ Most job opportunities are with local authorities.

▶ You would need the Rehabilitation Work (Visual Impairment) Diploma in higher education before you can start this work.

Housing

Homelessness officer

▶ Your work would involve dealing with individuals or families who are in crisis because they are homeless. This could be because of a family break-up, financial difficulties, release from prison or drug or alcohol abuse.

▶ You would interview homeless people to find out what their situation is, assess what help they need and what they can be offered. You would then find them somewhere to stay in suitable accommodation.

▶ Your work may involve liaising with social services, housing associations, the police, health authorities and other support organisations.

Hostel support workers/project worker

▶ You would support homeless people living in temporary accommodation.

▶ Your role would involve advising people on welfare benefits, housing, training and employment opportunities. You would also provide support and advice to help people prepare for living independently.

▶ You could be working with vulnerable adults, including people with mental health issues and drug or alcohol problems.

Housing adviser

▶ You would give advice and guidance to people who are experiencing housing difficulties. They might be homeless, unable to pay their mortgage or rent, need repairs, or be in a dispute with their landlord or neighbours.

▶ Your job would involve interviewing people to assess their problems and help them find solutions. You could get involved with mediating in disputes, for example between the person and their landlord.

▶ Your work would also include referring people to other support, for example social workers and housing officers. Housing advisers might work in advice centres or in hostels for people with special housing needs.

Community work

Community development worker

▶ In this role you would work closely with people in local communities and community organisations to identify problems and develop new community-based programmes.

▶ You might work on a project, for example to improve healthcare or get better access to services for vulnerable groups. Your work could focus on specific groups in a region, such as the homeless, the long-term unemployed or members of minority ethnic communities.

▶ As a community development worker you could work for local authorities, housing associations, NHS Trusts or in the voluntary and charity sector.

Community safety officer

▶ You role would focus on reducing crime and disorder and making the community where you work a safer place to live in.

▶ In this role you would help tackle issues such as crime and antisocial behaviour, drug abuse prevention, domestic abuse, housing, employment and regeneration.

▶ Working in partnership with the police and local voluntary organisations, you would put plans in place to reduce crime, such as making new housing estates safer by installing good lighting or CCTV cameras.

▶ Community safety officers are usually employed by local authorities.

Outreach worker

▶ You would support people in the community with additional needs, including homeless people, asylum seekers, unemployed people, people with mental health issues and people with disabilities.

▶ Your work would vary widely depending on your client group. Employment outreach workers, for example, help unemployed people to access training and job placement opportunities and support them back into work. Mental health outreach workers help people with long-term mental health issues to adapt to everyday life, and might provide personal, social and domestic care.

▶ You could work for a local authority or for a wide range of organisations within the voluntary and charity sector.

Probation

Probation staff work closely with related agencies such as the police and prisons. They work for the National Probation Service (NPS).

Probation officer

▶ You would work to protect the public and reduce crime by supervising offenders in the community.

▶ Your job would involve providing courts with advice and information on defendants, through preparing pre-sentence reports, and enforcing community orders made by the courts, such as carrying out unpaid work in the community.

▶ You could be working with prisoners during and after their sentence to help them in their resettlement and work directly with offenders to change their behaviour and reduce the risk of harm.

> 66 Probation officers may work with serious offenders, which can make the job emotionally demanding. 99

▶ Trainee probation officers have to be at least 20 years old and follow a two-year programme to become professionally qualified.

Probation service officer

▶ This is a similar job to the role of probation officers, but a probation service officer is not professionally qualified and only supervises low-risk offenders.

Supervisor

▶ You would manage unpaid work in the community that offenders are doing.

▶ Your job would involve encouraging offenders to learn practical skills that they can use to find a job.

Third sector

Volunteer manager

▶ You would be responsible for recruiting, training and looking after volunteers in your organisation.

▶ You would promote the volunteering opportunities available in your organisation, for example working on a community project or fundraising, in order to recruit new volunteers. You would then interview volunteers to assess their skills and qualities, and put together induction and training programmes for volunteers.

Charity fundraiser

▶ You would raise money for charities and related organisations. You would target potential donors including individuals, businesses, statutory bodies, trusts and communities.

▶ You would develop new fundraising activities, many of which will be events-based, as well as organising traditional activities such as house-to-house collections.

▶ Your role could also involve producing supporting materials, such as websites and newsletters to promote events, as well as giving talks and media interviews to raise awareness of the charity and its work.

JOBS THAT REQUIRE A HIGHER-LEVEL QUALIFICATION

This book looks at jobs you can move into without higher-level qualifications.

On the following two pages you will find details of jobs to show how you could move your career into more specialised professional roles through further qualifications and training.

JOBS REQUIRING HIGHER-LEVEL QUALIFICATIONS

Job	About	Qualification	More information	What jobs could lead into this role?
Social worker	You would work with vulnerable people who use social care services, helping them tackle the problems they face and find solutions. You could choose to specialise in working with a particular group of people, such as: ▲ older people ▲ people with mental health issues ▲ people with physical or learning difficulties, or sensory impairment.	A social work degree.	Visit the social work careers website at www.socialworkcareers.co.uk for information about getting into social work.	After gaining experience as a **community care officer**, you could go on to take a social work degree to train to be a social worker. It might be possible to do this part time while working. As a community care officer you would work in a social work team, helping social workers in their job. You would provide day-to-day support to adults who need additional support.
Occupational therapist	It would be your job to help people to overcome the effects of disability. You would put together treatment programmes to help people achieve as much as possible.	An occupational therapy degree.	Visit the British Association of Occupational Therapists website at www.baot.org.uk for more information.	With experience as an **occupational support worker**, you might decide to go on to take an occupational therapy degree and train to become an occupational therapist.

Job	About	Qualification	More information	What jobs could lead into this role?
	for themselves and to lead independent lives. You would work in hospitals and community settings, such as residential homes and day centres.			You might be able to do this part time while working. Occupational therapy support workers work directly with clients to encourage them to progress towards goals that have been agreed with the occupational therapist.
Counsellor	Counsellors help people explore their own solutions to their particular situation in a safe, confidential setting. They support clients by listening carefully and patiently, making observations and asking questions. There are generally more part-time than full-time jobs and counsellors could benefit from being able to work in other roles as well.	While there are no specific entry qualifications for this job, clients are less likely to choose a counsellor who does not have a recognised qualification. It is rare for someone to enter full-time counselling work before their mid-twenties.	A degree in social sciences, psychology or human sciences can be useful preparation for counselling training.	People who move into counselling have often worked in areas such as **social work, nursing** or **teaching** (all of which require higher qualifications) and have become experienced at working with people, before starting counselling training.

Quick recap!

✓ Remember, many roles in care work are emotionally as well as physically demanding.

✓ You will work with people from all walks of life; you need to keep an open mind and a positive attitude.

✓ There are currently lots of new opportunities being created in the adult guidance sector in particular.

CHAPTER 4
REAL LIVES 1

ZOE BENTON: SUPPORT WORKER

Zoe Benton is a support worker for the Move On Project at the Brandon Trust, an organisation that aims to provide greater independence and choices for people with learning disabilities.

As part of a team of support workers, Zoe provides on-site support at a house for adults with mild learning disabilities in Weston-super-Mare, Somerset. In addition to working full time, Zoe also volunteers as a care ambassador*, helping to promote the many career opportunities available in the care sector.

How did you get into this area of work?

I actually went to college to study dance, but I realised it wasn't for me and left not knowing what I wanted to do. I heard about the Move On Project and went to talk to the manager.

I first gained experience through 'bank work' – covering shifts when someone is off sick or away. When a full-time post became available, I applied and got the job. I've been in my role for about a year now.

What does your job involve?

My job is to help service users prepare for living independently. Service users come to live at the house (we have five living here at any one time) and we're there to help them to develop

> 66 We're there to help the clients to develop confidence with important life skills. 99

* The Care Ambassador Scheme is run in local areas.

confidence with important life skills such as dealing with money and bills, shopping and cooking.

After a year, we support them through a gradual 'move over' process into living independently.

We do things such as going out shopping with our service users and accompanying them to activities such as bowling and swimming. Our job is to provide support when our service users feel they need it. Paperwork is also a big part of my work because we need to keep detailed records of risk assessments for each service user.

> 66 Our job is to provide support when our service users feel they need it. 99

What are your hours like?

I work in shifts with one night's 'sleep-in' at the centre a week. My shift hours are 8.30am to 3.30pm, 1.30pm to 9pm or 8am to 4pm.

What sort of training have you had for your role?

I was given lots of training when I started the job, for example on health and safety and on how to complete and update all the required paperwork.

We need to be prepared to support the individual needs of our service users, so, for example, before we were joined by a service user with epilepsy, we received training on supporting people with this condition.

I'm just about to start my NVQ level 3 in Health and Social Care. This will take me 18 months.

What do you find most rewarding about your job?

It's great when service users are ready to move on to living independently. It's a good feeling to know I've helped them build their own lives. For example, one service user we helped now has his own flat and only needs a small amount of support each week with dealing with his bills. He comes back regularly to visit us!

What is the most challenging aspect of this work?

Lone working can be demanding when you're responsible for five service users. For example, if your service users are having a bad day, you need to be able to think on the spot and make a decision about how to respond to the situation. But that's the kind of know-how you develop through experience on the job.

> **66** It's great when service users are ready to move on to living independently. It's a good feeling to know I've helped them build their own lives. **99**

What sort of personal qualities do you think a person needs to do this job?

You need to be quite confident in yourself and be clear about what you need to do. You should also be patient and friendly. Being able to listen to people is also very important.

You also do regular voluntary work as a care ambassador. What does this involve?

Care ambassadors are part of a national Skills for Care scheme. The scheme promotes social care as an exciting career option. Care ambassadors visit schools, colleges and attend events to share their experience of working in social care roles.

I've been a care ambassador for six months and have been into secondary schools to tell them about the scheme and the care sector. I'm looking forward to gaining more experience in this role and going to conferences and into primary schools.

How would you like your career to develop in the future?

I'd like to go on to do the NVQ4 in Health and Social Care which would qualify me to become a care manager. I hope to continue working with people with learning difficulties.

TOP TIP!

If your service users are having a bad day, you need to be able to think on the spot and make a decision about how to respond to the situation.

What would you say to someone thinking about working in the care sector?

Look around at what jobs there are and think about what interests you. Find out about which organisations you might like to work for and try getting 'bank work' to gain some practical experience of the job.

CHAPTER 5
TOOLS OF THE TRADE

What kinds of skills and personal qualities do you need to succeed in the adult care, welfare and community sector?

WHAT DOES IT TAKE TO WORK WITH PEOPLE?

The social care sector is all about working with people. Whether you're working one to one in a person's home or managing activities for the residents of a care home, your job is about improving the lives of individuals.

TOP TIP!

In a sector where jobs often combine practical help with some level of emotional support, you need the right mix of hands-on and interpersonal skills.

Interpersonal skills

Respect

Respect for other people is an essential part of any job in social care. Whether it is your role to provide support, information or personal care, you need to have respect for your client's needs and point of view.

The focus of social care is on empowering people. Being respectful and non-judgemental is a big part of this.

The nature of the job also means it is essential to have an interest in other people. You'll need good listening skills and good overall communication skills.

You could be supporting clients with various needs, so you should be able to communicate well with different people. Working with people also involves maintaining a friendly and professional approach – even when you're having a tough day yourself!

A responsible approach

A responsible attitude is important in a role in which you could be supporting people on a regular basis. Whatever area of social care you work in, it is vital to be trustworthy and committed to meeting the needs of your clients. Many jobs in social care involve shift or evening or weekend work so you need to be motivated to attend work as scheduled. You will also need to take a mature, responsible approach to your work. You could be responsible for helping people manage their medication or take care of their bills.

> 66 Whatever area of social care you work in, it is vital to be trustworthy and committed to meeting the needs of your clients. 99

Confidence

As a professional in social care, you will find confidence is an important quality. You could be in a situation where a client is sharing personal information with you or where a service user is having a difficult day, and you need to be able to act appropriately.

You will also need to stay assertive when working with more challenging clients and to maintain a clear professional boundary at all times. For some jobs, you will also need the confidence to represent your clients in a formal setting.

Having life experience

This is probably the sector where life experience counts the most. Your experience of helping friends or relations through a difficult time could stand you in good stead for a career helping other people to move ahead with their lives. Practical experience or relevant voluntary experience can be a distinct advantage. In some jobs, such as counsellor, life experience and maturity are seen as essential by most employers.

Working with others

As well as working with your clients, a job in social care is likely to involve being part of a team, so you need to be flexible. Working with others could also include liaising with people from other organisations, such as the probation service, Connexions services and employers.

Working on your own

Even when you're part of a team you will need to be able to work independently. You could be supporting a group of clients on your own or visiting clients in their homes.

> 66 This is probably the sector where life experience counts the most. 99

Practical skills

The kinds of hands-on skills you need will depend on your actual job role. You should receive induction training when you start work. As well as helping you get to know

EXPLODE THAT MYTH!
If you're not very confident you won't be able to work in social care
It's true that a lot of the jobs in this sector require workers to be confident enough to make good decisions and stick to them and to hold their own when faced with a tricky situation with a client. But not everyone is going to be full of confidence when they start out in their first role. You will become more confident as you get used to working with other people. Remember to push yourself to tackle lots of different tasks and ask for help whenever you need it. You'll soon gain enough confidence to make your own decisions.

your employer and your role, this should give you an overview of the kinds of skills you'll need to do your job. There are likely to be even more opportunities to gain skills as you work in the future, thanks to the development of the new National Skills Academy for Social Care. You can find more about induction training and the academy in Chapter 8.

Being happy to travel around
How much you're on the move will depend on the nature of your job. It's obvious that an outreach support worker will be out a lot more than a key worker in a care home.

What is important is a willingness to be out and about when required, for example when supporting service users on a shopping trip, or visiting clients in different locations.

The ability to drive (along with a clean driving licence) could be useful for some roles, but is not essential for many areas of the sector.

Record keeping
This sector is all about providing professional support to people, so it is important to maintain clear, detailed records. This ensures that your service meets the required standards and allows you to keep track of the progress of each client. You should receive training on completing paperwork and updating records systems at your induction.

As you progress in your career, it is likely that the level of paperwork will increase, for example, as a care home manager you would be responsible for putting together staff rotas.

LEARN THE LINGO
Don't know what a word means? Turn to the Jargon Busters chapter on page 99 to find out.

IT skills

IT skills (or the willingness to develop them) are very useful for this sector. As we've already seen, keeping accurate, up-to-date records is essential. Increasingly, this type of work is done on computers.

Employers may have their own systems for managing client information. In some jobs, such as benefits adviser, you would need to access databases to provide information to your clients. You would be given training on this as part of your induction.

Retaining information

For many jobs in this sector, the support you offer your clients will involve providing information as and when they need it. This might be details of useful organisations for a client looking to move into employment, or the facts on debt management for someone seeking help with their finances. For these types of roles, you would need the ability to take in and remember a lot of information on specific subjects, such as benefits, rights and employment.

For most jobs, you would receive initial training on this, but you also need the ability to stay up to date with issues so that you can provide your clients with accurate information.

Health and physical fitness

A good level of health and physical fitness is important for working in social care. There's no doubt that for hands-on

> **❝** There's no doubt that for hands-on care work, you'll need to be fit. **❞**

care work, you'll need to be fit enough to support clients with activities such as personal care, washing and moving about via a hoist.

This means that some jobs in this sector may not be suitable for people with certain disabilities.

SKILLS YOU MIGHT GAIN BY WORKING IN THE SOCIAL CARE SECTOR

Social care involves a wide range of practical and professional skills. The specific skills you learn on the job will depend on your particular role. Some are essential; others are geared towards specific groups of clients.

They will also vary according to the level you work at. The kinds of skills you could learn while working could include:

- ▶ lifting and handling
- ▶ first aid
- ▶ risk assessment
- ▶ security in the workplace
- ▶ effective communication: spoken and written
- ▶ managing diabetes
- ▶ administering medication
- ▶ dealing with complaints
- ▶ supporting clients in different settings
- ▶ protecting vulnerable people

- ▶ policies and procedures
- ▶ confidentiality
- ▶ updating client records
- ▶ filing records
- ▶ reporting incidents
- ▶ activity planning
- ▶ fire safety
- ▶ organising staff rotas.

Quick recap!
- ✓ Life experience counts for a lot in this sector; much more than qualifications.
- ✓ It's really important that you can work well as part of a team of professionals, but don't forget you're likely to work with your clients one to one for a lot of the time. Make sure this is something you're comfortable with.
- ✓ In a role working with a vulnerable person, respect is the most important quality you can have.

Skills for Care Case Study

Caring Apprenticeships that make a real difference

James Murphy is 21 and has 9 GCSEs and 3 A levels. Since leaving college, James has had various jobs including bar work and working at a dairy. Struggling to find a permanent job with good career prospects, James was invited by his local Jobcentre Plus to an information session about social care. He was interested in social care but was not sure how you could get into the sector without experience. He was soon offered a social care apprenticeship, supporting Sean, 24, who has learning disabilities.

James says 'I'd never met, let alone worked with anyone with learning disabilities, it's very challenging but the experience is rewarding and I'm learning all the time'.

When James is with Sean he is learning in a practical way as Sean teaches him how he needs supporting. James also has support from the other members of the team who have been working with Sean for some time, and James knows that he can speak with them when he has any issues or questions on support, activities, or any other things that come up on a daily basis. James's valuable 'on-the-job' training is supplemented by attending college once a week, where he is doing a Technical Certificate and a NVQ level 2 in Health and Social Care.

'As I'm the same age as Sean it's great because I can support him with his favourite activities like bike riding, going to church and swimming, as well as personal tasks. I think we've got a real bond and a really good level of respect for each other'.

James admits that the job was difficult at first but feels that he's making a real difference to Sean's quality of life. James loves all aspects of the job and feels whilst Sean benefits, he feels good about himself too. He also celebrates the fact that he is making a difference.

James says 'There is no finer job, but you have to be 100% focused on the task in hand. I would recommend Apprenticeships to friends but you need to have patience and a genuine desire to help and care for people if you want to work in social care'.

James feels that he is fully supported as an apprentice and now wants to remain in social care with an aspiration of becoming a social worker in the future.

For more information about social care apprenticeships visit www.skillsforcare.org.uk/apprenticeships

CHAPTER 6
FAQs

By now you should have a much better idea of what working in the social care sector is all about and the opportunities it has to offer. But there are still lots of other things to think about when it comes to looking at a job in this area.

For example:

- ▶ who would you work for?
- ▶ where would you work?
- ▶ what kind of salary could you expect to earn?
- ▶ what would your career prospects be like?

In this chapter we will look at some of the most commonly asked questions about getting a job in the social care sector. This should help you decide whether or not this is the career path for you.

Q 66 How old do I have to be? 99

A Age requirements for working in social care are changing. The government has developed a more flexible approach to allowing 16–18-year-olds to provide personal care. Now they can do this as long as they're suitably trained and appropriately supervised.

If you are under 18 and want to work in personal care you should be undertaking, or have completed, an Apprenticeship in health and social care and have shown your line manager that you're capable of carrying out the necessary duties.

The Care Quality Commission regulates health and adult social care services and has information on national minimum standards – which include requirements relating to the employment and supervision of young people – on its website, www.cqc.org.uk.

Q **Who will I work for?** **"**

A Employers in this area include a huge range of organisations. You could work in the public sector, the private sector or the third sector (which includes charities, not-for-profit organisations and voluntary organisations). Social care workers, for example, might work in the public sector for a local authority, in the private sector for an agency, or in the third sector for a charity.

Local authorities are a major employer. They employ, for example, social workers, social care workers, advice workers, housing officers, community development workers and various kinds of support workers.

> ## ⚡ NEWSFLASH!
>
> Since it was set up in 1948 as part of the new welfare state, the NHS (National Health Service) has grown to become one of the largest employers in the world, along with the Chinese People's Liberation Army, the Indian railways and the Wal-Mart supermarket chain!

Possible employers include:

- ▶ agencies: for example recruitment agencies specialising in social care
- ▶ government agencies: such as the National Probation Service
- ▶ the third sector: voluntary organisations, not-for-profit organisations, local and national charities

▶ National Health Service (NHS) Trusts

▶ private organisations: such as residential establishments

▶ faith organisations

▶ individuals.

Q ❝ Where will I work? ❞
A You could work in a wide range of settings, including:

▶ people's homes

▶ residential and nursing care homes

▶ hostels for the homeless and supported housing schemes

▶ community centres and drop-in centres

▶ advice centres

▶ council offices

▶ hospitals: NHS and private

▶ prisons

▶ police stations.

Q ❝ Who will my clients be? ❞
A You will be helping people who, for whatever reason, need your support. Groups of people who may be in particular need of support include:

▶ people with physical and/or learning disabilities

▶ people with mental health issues

▶ people who are ill: both short-term and long-term

▶ older people

▶ people with alcohol and substance misuse problems

▶ offenders

▶ asylum seekers

▶ travellers

▶ homeless people

▶ people who have additional needs.

Q 66 **Who will I work with?** 99

A Your colleagues will vary depending on your particular job, but you will normally be part of a team working closely with other agencies and organisations to meet your client's needs.

> 66 Working with people means that no two days will ever be exactly the same. 99

In many jobs, you will be part of a team, but deal with clients on an individual basis. Your job may involve liaising with others on behalf of your clients, for example:

▶ health professionals

▶ council departments

▶ social services

▶ the courts

▶ the police service

▶ the probation service

▶ the voluntary sector

▶ housing associations.

Q 66 **Would I be doing the same kinds of activities every day?** 99

A Many social care jobs involve providing regular support to a specific person or client group. While this could entail doing similar kinds of activities on an ongoing basis, working with people means that no two days will ever be exactly the same. In some jobs you would visit people in their homes – this could include seeing up to six or seven people a day. In others, you could be supporting just a small number of people every week.

Q A 66 **Will I work 9 to 5?** 99

Again, this will vary widely depending on your particular job and the setting you are working in. As a full-time employee in a local authority you would work a standard 37-hour week, often with flexible working hours and opportunities for part-time working and job sharing.

A lot of people in the social care workforce choose to work part time. This is particularly the case with social care staff such as home care assistants, personal assistants and care assistants.

Personal assistants work a set number of hours a week, depending on their employer's needs. Some people work on short-term temporary contracts for agencies.

In some settings you would have to work unsocial hours. Workers in residential homes, supported housing schemes and homeless hostels work flexible shifts, including nights, bank holidays and weekends.

The home care service is available from 7am to 10.30pm, 365 days a year, so home care workers generally work in the evenings and on weekends.

In many jobs there will sometimes be a need for you to work in the evenings. Community development workers and housing officers, for example, might have to attend residents' meetings in the evenings, and social workers and outreach workers might have to visit clients outside conventional working hours. Advice and counselling centres could also have late opening times during the week.

Q 66 **How much travel does the job involve?** 99

A The amount of travelling you need to do depends entirely on your job. If you're based in a centre working with one group of people, you may go out three or four times a week to the local shopping centre or to the swimming baths.

> ⚡ **NEWSFLASH!**
>
> The care sector skills body Skills for Care estimates that by 2025, the adult social care workforce will increase by up to 80% to 2.5 million people.

Some roles specifically involve going out and about, for example, as a family outreach worker where visiting people in their homes would be a regular part of your job.

Q 66 **How much can I expect to earn?** 99

A The social care workforce spans many different sectors and employers and salaries can vary widely. Salaries can also vary between the private, public and third sectors. Here are some examples of salaries.

► A starting salary for a care worker is around £10,000.

► A money advice worker can start on around £16,000.

► Substance misuse workers in non-clinical settings may start on around £18,000 a year, rising to around £28,000 a year with experience.

► Community safety officers can start on around £17,000 a year and earn between £23,000 and £27,000 with experience.

► A care home manager can start earning around £19,000, with senior managers earning £37,000+.

Q 66 **What can I expect to get out of the job personally?** 99

A Supporting other people to live more independently, to make a positive change in their lives, or simply to grow in confidence is very rewarding. Your role is about making a difference to people's lives, which can make social care, welfare and community work a very fulfilling career choice.

Q
A
❝ What qualifications do I need? ❞

The qualifications you need depend on the type of job you choose to do. However, most social care jobs do not require you to have qualifications or training before you start. You would usually receive an induction and on-the-job training when you begin.

> ❝ Your role is about making a difference to people's lives. ❞

Your induction training would take place in the first 12 weeks of your new job and it would follow national standards relevant to your particular workplace. This training will equip you for your new role and also enable you to work towards the relevant NVQ.

You may also receive specialist training, for example as a welfare adviser. In a specialist area, such as benefits, it is likely that you would receive additional training on the job.

Q
A
❝ Will I have pre-employment checks? ❞

Yes. Pre-employment checks are essential in social care because employers have a duty to safeguard the people they provide services for. You will be in a position where you will be responsible for the welfare of vulnerable people and it is vital that your employer can check that you do not have criminal convictions that might suggest you are not suitable for this kind of work.

LEARN THE LINGO
Don't know what a word means? Turn to the Jargon Busters chapter on page 99 to find out.

Applicants are checked using data gathered by the Criminal Records Bureau (CRB), including relevant criminal convictions, cautions, police intelligence and other sources.

Q **❝ Are there good opportunities? ❞**

A If you have an interest in helping people, you'll find there is a huge choice of opportunities. This is a sector crying out for more employees. While starting salaries can be quite low, there are many different employers looking for reliable, responsible care professionals. This means there are opportunities in a range of settings, with many types of client group.

> ❝ This is a sector crying out for more employees. ❞

While many care jobs do not require formal qualifications before starting, this sector is a great route into other related areas with higher levels of pay, such as health work or nursing. Larger employers also provide the opportunity to complete professional qualifications on the job.

Q **❝ How easy is it to get promoted? ❞**

A Opportunities for promotion will vary according to your employer and area. With larger employers, such as local authorities, there will be a clear route for progressing your career. You should be able to aim towards gaining relevant qualifications. In other organisations, you may need to move around to progress into a supervisor or management role.

But with such a high demand for social care professionals, promotions prospects, with the right training, are generally good.

Q **❝ How is this sector viewed by the public? ❞**

A There's no doubt that the social care sector has been in the public eye a lot in recent times. There is growing concern about how social care can help tackle challenges such as deprived communities, child poverty and antisocial behaviour.

Check it out!

Take a look at www. socialcarecareers.co.uk for resources for working in this sector.

The sector needs responsible, motivated professionals to make a difference to the lives of many people.

Q ❝ **How can I find out more about working in this sector?** ❞

A You'll find details of helpful organisations at the back of this book. Depending on your age you may be able to arrange some practical experience through your school or college. If you are old enough you may be able to do some 'bank work' to gain practical experience of the job.

Quick recap!
- ✓ Although starting salaries can be low, most people working in this sector will tell you that it's the sense of fulfilment that is the most rewarding aspect of the job.
- ✓ Working in this sector is a great route into jobs such as nursing or working as a health worker.
- ✓ As you're working with a wide range of people, no day will be the same. This can be interesting and exciting, but remember, you need to be adaptable and react well to change.

CHAPTER 7
REAL LIVES 2

STEVE SUTTON: MONEY ADVISER

Steve Sutton works as a money adviser in the Money Advice Unit at the Liverpool Central Citizens Advice Bureau. The unit provides free advice on money and financial issues. Steve has been in his job for nearly four years.

Before this, he worked for 28 years in the credit industry, first as a call centre customer adviser and then as a call centre manager. After taking voluntary redundancy from this role, Steve decided he wanted to do something completely different and started working for Citizens Advice.

What is the purpose of your job?

I help clients deal with all sorts of debt issues. This includes what are called 'priority' debts such as mortgage, rent, council tax, fuel, TV licence; and unsecured lending such as credit card debt.

My job is to empower people to deal with the issues themselves or to give them the information they need to deal with the issues in the future.

What does your work involve?

People come into the unit with a wide range of debt issues. I meet with them individually and discuss their particular situation. That involves asking them for details such as their age, income, level of debt, and the amount they need to live on, so I can get a full picture of the situation,

> **"** My job is to empower people to deal with the issues themselves. **"**

and also (where applicable) ensure that they are receiving all the benefits to which they are entitled.

I often find that someone will come in with what they think is one urgent problem, only for more complex debt issues to emerge. I will work with the client to prioritise the debt issue, dealing with the most pressing issues first such as rent arrears and council tax. Then I'll give the client a full overview of their options.

These include things like putting together a short-term debt management plan, writing to creditors with reduced payment offers, suitability for insolvency options such as bankruptcy, debt relief orders (DRO) and, where appropriate, putting the client in touch with insolvency practitioners to arrange an IVA (Individual Voluntary Arrangement).

The client will then let me know which option they want to pursue and I'll take it from there. For example, I may represent the client at court for a bankruptcy hearing or contact creditors to discuss managing their debt. I can also do things such as applying to dedicated trust funds for assistance with a client's energy or water charges.

My job is also about highlighting the legal and other consequences of a client's actions, for example if they decide not to pay their rent or deal with their credit card debt.

Who are you there to help?

We will assist anyone regardless of income or personal circumstances. The key thing is that we are there to help people with pressing or difficult debt

> **"** The key thing is that we are there to help people with pressing or difficult debt problems. **"**

problems – not to give advice on things like getting the best financial deal on a credit card! The amount of assistance we provide depends on each client's circumstances. I will continue to work with a client until a debt agreement has been made and they are better able to manage and understand their financial affairs.

What sort of training have you had for your role?

When I started my job, I had intensive training on all aspects of money and debt over a period of four to five months. This covered things like credit card debt, insolvency, mortgage arrears and the Consumer Credit Act.

What is the most rewarding aspect of your job?

Feedback from clients is very rewarding, as is knowing that I have helped people ease their money worries.

What are the more challenging parts of your job?

It can be demanding trying to put across a client's case to their creditors. You need to be skilled in the art of negotiation. I have to be able to put forward a decent case for the client when I'm representing them in court, in front of a judge. You don't always win the case! All you can do is get as many relevant facts as you can and put together as compelling a case as possible.

What kind of personality do you need to do this job?

You need to be fairly outgoing and very open minded. You should be comfortable working with people from all walks of life and with people with different needs, and not be judgemental. That means being adaptable.

Steve's top tip
66 I think it's also important to be approachable with a relaxed manner so you put people at their ease. 99

CHAPTER 8
TRAINING AND QUALIFICATIONS

This sector is very varied – and so are the qualifications and training needed to progress in it. You can move into some jobs without formal qualifications: your people skills and enthusiasm will be more important than specific qualifications. This is particularly true if you are looking to start out in an unqualified, supervised role, such as a care assistant, and then gain qualifications on the job.

> 66 Your people skills and enthusiasm will be more important than specific qualifications. 99

But in order to progress, and for some college courses and Apprenticeship schemes, it is an advantage (or a must) to have at least four or five GCSEs (grades A*–C), preferably including English, or the equivalent.

For other jobs you'll need a higher-level qualification to apply, such as a diploma in higher education or a degree. These jobs include social work, occupational therapy and rehabilitation officer (visual impairment).

While there may be no set entry requirements for certain jobs, many employers will be looking at your ability to do on-the-job training and take further qualifications, so it is important to achieve the best qualifications you can while you are still at school.

After school, you may also want to consider taking a relevant course at college, or you may decide to take an Apprenticeship and gain qualifications on the job. Take a look at the following qualifications.

DIPLOMA IN SOCIETY, HEALTH AND DEVELOPMENT (SHD)

Diplomas are a new qualification for 14–19-year-olds that are increasingly available in schools and colleges. They bring together:

- ▶ applied learning
- ▶ academic study
- ▶ hands-on experience in the workplace.

They aim to provide young people with the skills and knowledge to set them on their way to finding a job or a route into higher education.

The Diploma in SHD has been available since September 2008. It is designed to provide young people with an understanding of health, community justice, social care and children's services and to help them develop the skills they need to work in all these areas.

The Diploma in SHD is offered at levels 1, 2 and 3 and is aimed at 14–19-year-olds of all abilities.

Level	Equivalent to	Work experience
1	4 or 5 GCSEs.	10 days' work placement.
2	5 or 6 good GCSEs.	10 days' work placement.
3	3 A levels.	20 days' work placement in at least two sectors.

The Diploma in SHD is very flexible.

▶ At levels 2 and 3 you can choose to combine the qualification with other GCSEs and A levels.

▶ You can move on from SHD to an Apprenticeship, employment, A levels or into higher education.

▶ The SHD will help you gain first-hand experience of the world of work, with a taster of four occupations and the range of sectors they are found in.

▶ The SHD can lead to a wide range of jobs in the social care workforce, from care assistant to social worker, and from police community support officer to probation officer.

Check it out!
www.skillsforhealth.org.uk/diploma.

QUALIFICATIONS IN HEALTH AND SOCIAL CARE

Vocational qualifications in health and social care are available at various levels, giving you a gateway to many different careers and courses.

A health and social care course at level 2, for example, could lead to jobs such as care assistant, working with older people or people with disabilities or to a level 3 qualification.

Level 3 courses offered at colleges include the Applied A level Health and Social Care (Single or Double Award) and the National Diploma in Health and Social Care. After this course you could move on to higher education and a degree such as social work or occupational therapy, or you could look directly for work in the health and social care sector.

While you're still at school you may also be able to opt for a GCSE in Health and Social Care (Double Award) which will give you a good grounding in the subject.

APPRENTICESHIPS

Thinking about leaving school and going straight into work? You may be interested in applying for an Apprenticeship. Apprenticeships provide 16–24-year-olds with a mixture of on- and off-the-job training while they are being paid.

Check it out!
www.apprenticeships.org.uk

► As employees, apprentices work alongside experienced staff to gain job-specific skills.

► They also receive off-the-job training, usually on a day-release basis, with a local training provider (such as a college) to acquire the knowledge to support their practical skills.

► An Apprenticeship may take anything from 12 to 24 months or longer to complete.

► Entry requirements vary and you'll need to discuss these with the individual training provider and employer.

► The table opposite gives details of the two levels of Apprenticeships that are available in England.

Apprenticeship	Who is it for?	What can it lead to?
Apprenticeships at level 2	People who want to work towards an NVQ level 2.	An ideal pathway to Advanced Apprenticeships and further education programmes, which can help open up new career opportunities.
Advanced Apprenticeships at level 3	People who want to work towards an NVQ level 3.	Suitable for people who show the ability to progress to positions at a supervisory level.

The table below gives details of Apprenticeships that could lead to jobs in the social care sector.

Apprenticeship	What does it cover?	What does it involve?	What could it lead to
Health and Social Care	A wide range of job roles within the health and social care fields.	You could choose to be an apprentice in social care where you would be helping people with a particular need, such as disabled people or older people. You could, for example, be a personal assistant helping people with their everyday lives.	Taking the Advanced Apprenticeship would be a good step towards a management role in a care home.
Advice and Guidance	You would learn advice and guidance	You'll need to be a good listener.	You could be giving advice and guidance

(*Continued*)

Apprenticeship	What does it cover?	What does it involve?	What could it lead to?
	skills that you could use in a range of sectors, from housing to adult guidance.		face to face in an advice centre or over the phone on an advice line.
Community Development	A good choice if you're interested in social change and making a difference.	As an apprentice you'll learn how to: identify a community's needs and problems; organise events; raise public awareness; manage budgets; and raise funds.	This Apprenticeship could lead to a job as a community development worker.
Community Justice	This Advanced Apprenticeship is for anyone who wants to improve their community by supporting vulnerable people.	You could be working with people with drug and alcohol problems, or with offenders, or with people who are concerned with safety in their community. You'll need to be able to communicate with different types of people.	A good step towards a number of jobs, such as substance misuse worker, probation officer, probation services officer, and community safety officer.

NATIONAL VOCATIONAL QUALIFICATIONS (NVQS)

You will study for NVQs if you are taking an Apprenticeship. You will also be expected to work towards them in many jobs.

The basics

▶ NVQs (and Scottish Vocational Qualifications – SVQs) are work-based qualifications that show that you are competent to do your job.

▶ There are no exams. You're assessed for your NVQs while you work.

▶ NVQs are available at different levels and in different subjects, depending on your job role and responsibilities, right up to management level.

▶ The time taken to complete an NVQ is flexible, although on average they take a year. NVQs are available to full-time, part-time, paid and voluntary workers in the social care workforce.

FOUNDATION DEGREES

The basics

▶ Foundation degrees are work-related higher education qualifications. They combine academic study with work-based learning.

▶ They allow students that are already employed to study and get ahead in their career while working. Courses are delivered by colleges and universities and have flexible learning arrangements.

▶ They normally take two years full time or up to three years part time to complete.

▶ At the end of a Foundation degree course, students have the opportunity to continue, and 'top-up' to an honours degree, which usually takes one year full time or two years part time.

> **Check it out!**
> www.findfoundationdegree.co.uk

▶ There are Foundation degrees relating to many job roles in adult care, welfare and community work.

VOLUNTEERING

Hands-on practical experience can be very helpful in developing a career in this sector. In fact, many people gain voluntary experience before choosing to move into paid work. Some of the professionals who share their stories in this book suggest practical experience as a helpful route into this job area. Volunteers make an important contribution to the social care, welfare and community sector.

Key things to keep in mind are: the kind of voluntary work you would like to do; the time you have to spare; and whether you can gain any practical skills and relevant training whilst volunteering.

Finding out about voluntary work

National volunteering bodies such as Volunteering England and Community Service Volunteers offer information on voluntary placements. You can find out more by visiting their websites.

▶ Your local Council for Voluntary Service (CVS) can give you information on opportunities in your area. You can usually visit them in person to discuss what you would like to do.

▶ Local Connexions services can provide details of volunteering opportunities for young people. Schools and colleges may also have information about volunteering or have arrangements to work with local charities.

▶ Individual organisations may also seek voluntary support directly. You can find information on their websites.

Examples of volunteering opportunities include the following.

▶ Care in the home volunteer: working for a national charity, helping people to regain their independence at home after a stay in hospital.

▶ IT buddy: supporting residents at a national charity's residential home, helping them to gain confidence and have fun while using the computer.

▶ Care support volunteer: providing information and support to the families of drug and alcohol users across a local authority area.

Whatever you choose to do, as a volunteer you must go through the relevant safety checks and a preparatory induction or training period.

LEARN THE LINGO
Don't know what a word means? Turn to the Jargon Busters chapter on page 99 to find out.

JOB-SPECIFIC QUALIFICATIONS AND TRAINING

Take a look at the qualifications and training in the following sections, which relate to the job roles outlined in Chapter 3.

Adult care
Social care worker
What you need
You won't necessarily need specific academic qualifications to start in this role, although qualifications in health and social care and experience of working with people would be useful.

What the training involves

As a social care worker you would have induction training in the first 12 weeks of the job. Induction training gives you professional recognition and prepares you to work unsupervised with clients in a safe, effective and caring manner.

What's next?

You may then go on to work towards NVQs in Health and Social Care at levels 2 and 3, which will help if you want to get promotion. Senior home care workers and team leaders in care homes, for example, normally have NVQ level 2 and 3, or are working towards NVQ level 3.

Once you've gained a level 3 qualification there's even more scope for progression. You could move up into more senior positions and take further training and qualifications whilst working, such as an NVQ level 4 in Health and Social Care or a Foundation degree in Health and Social Care.

Check it out!
www.socialcarecareers.co.uk

Residential care home manager

What you need

At least two years' experience managing a relevant care setting, and qualifications, such as a relevant NVQ at level 4, or a social work or nursing degree.

What's next?

Managers and deputy mangers can work towards NVQ level 4 in Leadership and Management for Care Services.

Qualified social worker
What you need
A degree in social work. The full-time degree course lasts three years, but you could also study for it part time or by distance learning. An NVQ in Health and Social Care at level 3 or 4, plus extensive social care work experience, might gain you entry to the degree course.

Some employers offer an employment-based route for their own employees working in social care roles. You would be supported by your employer and study part time.

What's next?
Practising social workers can go on to take specialised postgraduate training as part of their career development. See www.socialworkcareers.co.uk for more information.

Community care officer
What you need
You might not need formal qualifications, but experience of working in a caring setting could be required.

What's next?
You could work towards Health and Social Care NVQ level 3 and go on to take a relevant Foundation degree. This job will give you really good experience if you're thinking of applying for the social work degree and going on to train as a social worker.

Welfare
Housing officer
What you need
You don't necessarily need specific qualifications as entry requirements vary. Some employers might look for A levels

or the equivalent, or even a degree in housing. Others might look for relevant work experience in housing.

Experience in tenants' associations or similar community roles would be useful. You might be able to enter this work through a housing apprenticeship.

What's next?
As a housing officer you could work towards a range of professional qualifications to help develop your career.

Community support roles

Community development worker
What you need
Roles in this area vary widely and so do entry qualifications – from no specific qualifications to a degree. You will often need to have some work experience (paid or voluntary) of community work.

> 66 Work experience in a job where you're dealing with people would be useful. 99

You might be able to get into this work through an Apprenticeship in community development.

What's next?
In this job you could work towards NVQs in community development work and go on to study for a Foundation degree and then a degree in community development.

Community safety officer
What you need
Entry requirements vary. Some authorities might ask for a degree or equivalent qualification, and experience in a related area, such as probation work.

You might be able to enter this work through an Apprenticeship in community justice.

INDUCTION TRAINING

When you start work in social care, you should receive induction training. This should help you get to know your employer and your role and give you an overview of the kinds of skills you'll need to do your job.

In social care you should complete your Skills for Care Common Induction standards within the first 12 weeks of starting your job. You should receive support from your manager and possibly also your colleagues.

Your induction could also include support from external trainers or you might need to attend courses outside your workplace. Professional induction training is designed to lead on to qualifications such as NVQs.

What's next?
In the job you could work towards relevant NVQs and go on to take a Foundation degree in crime and community safety.

Police community support officer (PCSO)
What you need
You won't need any specific qualifications, but work experience in a job where you're dealing with people and some experience of community service would be useful.

What's next?
Working as a PCSO is an ideal way of gaining experience if you're considering a career in the police service, and many PCSOs go on to train to become police officers.

Substance misuse worker
What you need
There are no set entry requirements to start work as a substance misuse worker, although many employers will

Access to . . . care, welfare and community work

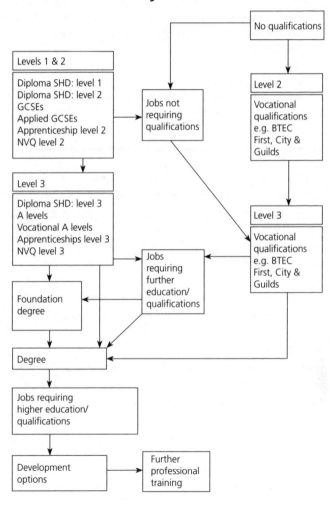

look for work experience in a health, social care or criminal justice setting.

NVQs in health and social care and experience of working with vulnerable people, either paid or voluntary, would be useful. You might be able to get into this work through an Apprenticeship in community justice.

What's next?
You could go on to work towards vocational awards in working with substance misuse at levels 3 and 4.

LOOKING AHEAD

National Skills Academy for Social Care

The National Skills Academy for Social Care is a new organisation for the care sector. Launched in late 2009, the academy will be supported by £6 million in public funding over the next three years. It's aims are:

▶ developing more skills and training opportunities for people working in social care

▶ offering support to service users who employ personal assistants

▶ increasing the number of people taking up Apprenticeships at foundation and advanced levels

▶ increasing the number of adults qualified to at least NVQ level 2 and level 3.

New social care Apprenticeships

The government wants to create 50,000 new social care Apprenticeships. The scheme, administered by JobCentre Plus, is under review but it should be available to young people who have been unemployed for at least one year. Employers should receive a £1,500 subsidy to take on new trainees. Existing Apprenticeship schemes will also be expanded.

Quick recap!

✓ Most employers in this sector tend to look for hands-on experience rather than qualifications in their candidates.

✓ If you want to earn while you are training, an Apprenticeship is a great idea.

✓ The government is investing a lot of money in training in this area of work, so now is a fantastic time to think about getting a job in the social care sector.

CHAPTER 9
REAL LIVES 3

ALISON PENNINGTON: RESETTLEMENT OUTREACH WORKER

Alison Pennington is a resettlement outreach worker for the Peasholme Charity in York. The charity provides crisis and resettlement services to help homeless single people gain access to accommodation and move ahead with their lives. Alison's role is to provide support to clients moving on from supported housing to living independently in housing provided by the council or through a housing association. Resettlement support generally lasts for 12 months. Alison might visit clients twice a week or fortnightly, depending on their needs. She has been in this role for two years.

What's a typical day in your job like?

There is no such thing as a typical day in my job! I am generally out of the office around 70% of my working week. I usually do about two to three visits a day. Some days I'm not in the office at all because I'm doing back-to-back visits to clients – sometimes at different ends of York!

On a visit I will discuss with the client the kind of support they might need. This varies because every client is different. They might need help with dealing with the financial side of things, such as bills or housing benefits, or with looking for work. When tenants first move into their flat, they often need support with finding furniture and carpets.

> **❝** It's good to feel that, with our support, [people] are better able to manage the challenges they might come up against and to move beyond homelessness. **❞**

What else does your work involve?

My office time is usually taken up with completing contact notes and other paperwork on the computer. I also spend half a day a week doing office cover, taking calls and queries from tenants.

Occasionally I will go to open days with other agencies, such as housing associations and the job centre, to keep up to date with the support that is available to our tenants.

What sort of training have you had for your role?

I do a lot of on-the-job training. I have access to training courses provided by our local council and I also do training provided through a company that specialises in training for professionals working with homeless people. This covers issues such as mental health, first aid, personal safety for lone workers and safeguarding vulnerable adults.

What do you enjoy most about your job?

I enjoy seeing people move on through the resettlement process. It's good to feel that, with our support, they are better able to manage the challenges they might come up against and to move beyond homelessness.

What are the challenges of your work?

I think the main challenge of the role is supporting and enabling people to make difficult changes in their lives in order for them to achieve their aims.

> **❝** The challenge is to remember that clients are still finding their feet and they need to do things their own way. **❞**

It is great to see someone make a change, for example moving away from offending into paid employment.

It can be frustrating to give advice to a client and for it not to be taken. But the challenge is to remember that clients are still finding their feet and they need to do things their own way. My job is to be there to support them through this process.

The physical nature of my job can be demanding. I travel to clients by bike or on the bus. That means dealing with traffic and having the energy to go out to appointments in all weathers. Cycling to appointments in the snow can be tough!

Did you always know you wanted to work in this sector?

I actually used to work in science – in a laboratory, after gaining a degree in biology. I realised this wasn't right for me and I started doing voluntary work in a homeless hostel in York.

This gave me a great insight into the work and also helped me get my first job at the Peasholme Charity. I started off working in a day centre for homeless people and then progressed into my current role.

What sort of personality do you need for this type of work?

It's essential to be able to listen well, to really take in what someone is telling you and to show that you understand what they're saying. Sometimes I might be told difficult things about a client's experiences and I still need to listen and provide a supportive, professional response.

You also need to be able to stay calm when you're with a client who is going through a crisis, such as an urgent problem with their finances. But this comes with experience in the job.

Patience is important, as is a good level of energy! I have also found that being flexible is essential. You might have a plan for the day, but things can change fast, for example if a client cancels an appointment or needs additional support urgently. You have to be able to respond fast and prioritise your activities.

I also think that a sense of humour is important! It sounds obvious, but you have to like people and be interested in how individuals develop the skills they need. There's always something new to learn about people in this job.

What kind of practical skills do you need?

IT skills are useful because I have to manage all my paperwork on the computer. A good knowledge of the different organisations that are there to support your clients is also helpful. You need to be able to hold a lot of information in your head and have a broad knowledge base to give clients the information they need – as and when they need it. There's a lot of information to be aware of on issues such as housing, employment, utilities and benefits.

> **Alison's top tip**
> 66 Try and gain some voluntary experience in a relevant organisation. Look at particular areas that interest you and don't be afraid to try different things out to develop your understanding of what's right for you. 99

CHAPTER 10
THE LAST WORD

Now you know about the many different jobs and career opportunities this sector has to offer. But is it the right choice for you?

After finding out from this book about working in social care, welfare and the community, you should have a better idea of whether it is for you. You should also have a clearer idea of the kinds of jobs on offer and what the work involves.

You now know more about the kinds of personal and practical skills you need. As you have seen, this is a very varied sector, with opportunities in all kinds of settings. It's also a sector where it is possible to make a difference to people and to local communities. But perhaps you're still wondering whether it is for you. That's fine, because this book is a starting point for finding out more.

There are plenty of ways to learn more about working in this sector. You can contact the organisations listed in Chapter 11. You could look out for opportunities to visit (with appropriate permission) social care, welfare or community workplaces yourself – or even gain some practical experience.

With more detailed information you can start answering any further questions you may have, for example:

- ▶ would you be able to move into the sector with your current skills or qualifications? If not, what additional training might you need?

- ▶ are there flexible options to allow you to gain practical, paid or voluntary experience, such as part-time work or a one-off work placement?

- ▶ what are the opportunities for progressing from an entry-level job?

- ▶ what kind of training and development support do you receive once you start work?

With so much going on in this sector, it is likely you'll need to know more. Whatever questions you have, you'll find information about developing a career in social care, welfare and community work from the organisations listed in the next chapter.

If you've made it this far through the book, you should know whether social care, welfare and community work is right for you. But before getting in touch with the professional bodies listed in the next chapter, here's a final, fun checklist to see if you have chosen wisely.

Do you enjoy being around people?	☐ Yes	☐ No
Are you able to stay calm and friendly when you're under pressure?	☐ Yes	☐ No
Are you confident about meeting different types of people?	☐ Yes	☐ No

Are you comfortable dealing with paperwork such as forms?	☐ Yes	☐ No
Are you able to adapt when things don't go to plan?	☐ Yes	☐ No
Can you communicate information orally and in writing?	☐ Yes	☐ No
Are you comfortable doing hands-on tasks such as helping with washing up or cooking?	☐ Yes	☐ No
Would you describe yourself as outgoing?	☐ Yes	☐ No
Do you have a mature, responsible attitude?	☐ Yes	☐ No
Do you follow working processes and procedures well?	☐ Yes	☐ No

If you answered 'Yes' to all these questions, congratulations – you've chosen the right career! If you answered 'No' to any of these questions, a career in adult social care, welfare and community work may not be for you. However, there are still plenty of other jobs in this sector which may suit you better, such as a catering role in a care setting or an administrative job in a local authority.

CHAPTER 11
FURTHER INFORMATION

Listed in this section are contact details for organisations that can give you further information about education, training and job opportunities in care, welfare and community work.

GENERAL INFORMATION ON THE SECTOR AND THE JOBS

Apprenticeships
www.apprenticeships.org.uk
Detailed information on Apprenticeships.

City & Guilds
Tel: 020 7294 2800
www.cityandguilds.com

This site details the up-to-date qualifications available for the care sector. You can also use this site to find a City & Guilds approved training centre.

Connexions
www.connexions-direct.com

Careers information for young people, with links to local Connexions offices.

Criminal Records Bureau (CRB)

CRB Registration Team, PO Box 110, Liverpool L69 3EF
Registration information line: 0870 909 0822
www.crb.homeoffice.gov.uk

The CRB's aim is to help organisations in the public, private and voluntary sectors by identifying candidates who may be unsuitable to work with children or other vulnerable members of society.

Department for Children, Education, Lifelong Learning and Skills (DCELLS)

(Replaces Education and Learning Wales)
Tel: 0300 060 3300
http://wales.gov.uk/

The organisation responsible for funding and planning education and training for people aged over 16 years old in Wales.

Department for Employment and Learning

Tel: 028 9025 7777
www.delni.gov.uk

The organisation responsible for funding and planning education and training for people aged over 16 years old in Northern Ireland.

Edexcel

One90 High Holborn, London WC1V 7BH
www.edexcel.com

Information on a wide range of qualifications.

Foundation Degrees
www.findfoundationdegree.co.uk

Information on Foundation degrees.

Lifelong Learning
www.lifelonglearning.co.uk

Information on Career Development Loans – deferred repayment bank loans to pay for vocational learning or education.

New Deal
www.direct.gov.uk/Jobseekers

Information for people claiming benefits about help and support available to help them look for work, including training and job preparation.

Scottish Funding Council
Donaldson House, 97 Haymarket Terrace, Edinburgh
EH12 5HD
Tel: 0131 313 6500
www.sfc.ac.uk

The organisation responsible for funding and planning education and training for people aged over 16 years old in Scotland.

Society, Health and Development Diploma
http://shd.skillsforhealth.org.uk/

Detailed information on the new Society, Health and Development Diploma.

UCAS
www.ucas.com

Information on degree courses in the UK.

Young People's Learning Agency
Cheylesmore House, Quinton Road, Coventry CV1 2WT
Tel: 0845 337 2000
www.ypla.gov.uk

The organisation responsible for funding and planning education and training for people aged 16–19 years old in England. In Scotland this work is undertaken by the Scottish Funding Council; in Wales by the Department for Children, Education, Lifelong Learning and Skills (DCELLS); and in Northern Ireland by the Department for Employment and Learning (see separate entries).

TRAINING AND JOB OPPORTUNITIES

Care Council for Wales
South Gate House, Wood Street, Cardiff CF10 1EW
Tel: 029 2022 6257
www.ccwales.org.uk

Promotes high standards of conduct and practice among social care workers and high standards in their training.

Care Quality Commission
St Nicholas Building, St Nicholas Street, Newcastle upon Tyne NE1 1NB
Tel: 0300 061 6161
www.cqc.org.uk

The independent regulator of health and social care in England.

Department for Education
Castle View House, East Lane, Runcorn WA7 2GJ
Tel: 0870 001 2345
www.education.gov.uk

Government department which leads the network of people who work with or for children and young people.

INFORMATION ON SPECIFIC JOB AREAS

Community development

Community Development Exchange
Scotia Works, Leadmill Road, Sheffield S1 4SE
Tel: 0114 241 2760
www.cdx.org.uk

The UK-wide membership organisation for community development.

Community Development Foundation
Head Office, Unit 5, Angel Gate, 320–26 City Road, London EC1V 2PT
Tel: 020 7833 1772
www.cdf.org.uk

Public body and charity which provides community development expertise and delivery.

Housing

Chartered Institute of Housing
Octavia House, Westwood Way, Coventry CV4 8JP
Tel: 024 7685 1700
www.cih.org/careers

The professional body for people who work in housing.

Justice

Skills for Justice
Centre Court, Atlas Way, Sheffield S4 7QQ
Tel: 0114 261 1499
www.skillsforjustice.com

The Sector Skills Council and standards-setting body for the justice sector.

Social care

General Social Care Council
Goldings House, 2 Hay's Lane, London SE1 2HB
Tel: 020 7397 5100
www.gscc.org.uk

The social care workforce regulator in England.

National Care Forum
3 The Quadrant, Coventry CV1 2DY
Tel: 024 7624 3619
www.nationalcareforum.org.uk

Represents the interests of not-for-profit health and social care providers in the United Kingdom.

National Skills Academy for Social Care
2nd Floor, Goldings House, 2 Hay's Lane, London SE1 2HB
Tel: 020 7397 5629
www.skillsacademyforsocialcare.org.uk

The National Skills Academy for Social Care is the first welfare-related skills academy in the National Skills Academy network.

Scottish Social Services Council
Compass House, 11 Riverside Drive, Dundee DD1 4NY
Tel: 01382 207101
www.sssc.uk.com

The organisation responsible for registering people who work in social services in Scotland.

Skills for Care
West Gate, 6 Grace Street, Leeds LS1 2RP
Tel: 0113 245 1716
www.skillsforcare.org.uk

The employer-led authority on the training standards and development needs of social care staff in England.

Social Care Association
350 West Barnes Lane, Motspur Park KT3 6NB
Tel: 020 8949 5837
www.socialcareassociation.co.uk

A UK membership organisation that promotes good practice in social care and shares these ideas in practice guides, which are available to members.

Welfare

Citizens Advice
www.citizensadvice.org.uk

Membership organisation that provides training and support to the 416 Citizens Advice Bureaux across England and Wales and the 22 bureaux in Northern Ireland. The Citizens Advice service helps people resolve their legal, money and other problems by providing free information and advice and influencing policy makers.

Be protected
Be supported
Be informed
Be assisted
Be heard
Be cared for

The UK professional body for workers in
Support, Care & Assistance

Contact **SCA** today to find out how
to become a member

☎ **020 8949 5837**
🖰 **sca@socialcaring.co.uk**

www.socialcareassociation.co.uk

Institute of Money Advisers
Stringer House, 34 Lupton Street, Leeds LS10 2QW
Tel: 0845 094 2384
www.i-m-a.org.uk

The only professional body acting solely for money advisers in England, Wales and Northern Ireland.

Volunteering

Community Service Volunteers
237 Pentonville Road, London N1 9NJ
Tel: 020 7278 6601
www.csv.org.uk

Leading volunteering and training charity.

Do-it
www.do-it.org.uk

The only national database of volunteering opportunities in the UK.

National Council for Voluntary Organisations
Regent's Wharf, 8 All Saints Street, London N1 9RL
Tel: 0800 279 8798
www.ncvo-vol.org.uk

The largest umbrella body for the voluntary and community sector in England.

Scottish Council for Voluntary Organisations
Mansfield Traquair Centre, 15 Mansfield Place, Edinburgh EH3 6BB
Tel: 0131 556 3882
www.scvo.org.uk

The national body representing the voluntary sector in Scotland.

Volunteering England
Regents Wharf, 8 All Saints Street, London N1 9RL
Tel: 0845 305 6979
www.volunteering.org.uk

Works to support and increase the quality, quantity, impact and accessibility of volunteering throughout England.

USEFUL BOOKS

Careers 2011, Trotman, 2010.
Compass: The Complete Guide to Careers in Social Work and Social Care, Compass, 2009.

OTHER SOURCES OF INFORMATION

www.communitycare.co.uk
Social care jobs and news.

www.greatsocialcare.co.uk
Home and residential homecare jobs and social housing jobs.

***Guardian* newspaper**
Public sector job section every Wednesday.

www.lgjobs.com
The official government job site advertising council vacancies.

www.probation.homeoffice.gov.uk
Information about the National Probation Service.

www.scie-socialcareonline.org.uk
The UK's most complete range of information and research on all aspects of social care.

www.socialcarecareers.co.uk
Careers helpline: 0300 123 1100

The Department of Health's Social Care website. Includes information on issues and matters relating to social care work and links to vacancy websites and downloadable careers booklets.

***Social Caring* magazine**
Journal of the Social Care Association.

www.socialworkcareers.co.uk
Careers helpline: 0300 123 1100

The Department of Health's Social Work website. Includes information on careers in social work.

CHAPTER 12
JARGON BUSTERS

Connexions services

Connexions is a national network of organisations that offers support to young people aged 13 to 19 years old. It provides advice and information about careers, jobs, learning, health, relationships, money and more. Young people can access support through local Connexions centres, online or over the phone. You can find more information at www.connexions-direct.com.

Looked-after children

Children in public care, who are placed in residential homes, with parents or other relations or with foster carers. It is the way care professionals now refer to children in care.

National Care Service

The government is developing a National Care Service aimed at making it easier, fairer and more affordable for people to have the care services they need.

Skills for Care Common Induction Standards

Standards for people entering social care and people changing roles or employers in adult social care. They were introduced in 2005 by Skills for Care, the development body for the adult social care workforce in England. The 12-week CIS induction period allows care workers to give high-quality care and support and gives them recognition for their work. It also helps to prepare them for moving on to NVQ health and social care programmes.

Third sector

Third sector is a general name for the sector made up of charity, voluntary, community and non-government organisations.

White Paper

A report produced by the government in preparation for proposing a new law about a specific issue such as social care, health or energy. It sets out the benefits of the proposed new law and the actions needed to achieve it.